FIXER UPPER FUNDING

Renovation Lending Revealed

David Lewis -- 1st ed.
ISBN: 978-1-7323763-4-2

The Publisher has strived to be as accurate and complete as possible in the creation of this book.

This book is not intended for use as a source of legal, business, accounting or financial advice. All readers are advised to seek the services of competent professionals in legal, business, accounting, and finance field.

In practical advice books, like anything else in life, there are no guarantees of income or results made. Readers are cautioned to rely on their own judgement about their individual circumstances to act accordingly.

While all attempts have been made to verify information provided in this publication, the Publisher assumes no responsibility for errors, omissions, or contrary interpretation of the subject matter herein. Any perceived slights of specific persons, peoples, or organizations are unintentional.

Table of Contents

INTRODUCTION

If you are considering purchasing a "fixer-upper" to convert into your dream home, you probably have a lot of questions like...

"Can I obtain renovation and purchase funds in one, simple loan?"

"What types of work will a renovation loan allow me to perform?"

"Can a renovation loan benefit me when it comes to a home I currently own?"

You're not alone. In today's housing market, there is a large inventory of homes that could be just right for you, but may need some updates or renovations.

Understanding how to obtain these homes with one loan can help make that "diamond in the rough" property become a place for you and your family to grow and thrive. I have successfully helped many homebuyers to do just that. One thing I've realized is that there are a lot of common questions and concerns in the beginning.

You see, I've noticed quite a few myths and misconceptions surrounding renovation lending. While some of these might just be harmless misinformation, others can have a big impact on your home buying decisions when they are simply not true..

I've also seen a lot of people make some costly mistakes that could have easily been avoided if they just had the right information and answers to their questions.

That's why I wrote this short book – to help you navigate your way through the maze and discover the secrets to successful renovation lending.

No fluff, no technical jargon, only straight information you want to know and NEED to know before making the decision to purchase a home. I'll cover the benefits, pros and cons, and answer the most pressing questions I get about renovation lending. I'll also dispel the biggest myths and misconceptions about renovation loans as well as share the most common mistakes people make and how those mistakes can be avoided.

Let me be clear. While this book is packed full of valuable information about the most common issues you may be facing, it doesn't have all the answers. That would be impossible because the truth is there is no single right answer for everyone.

Even though the differences may be small, every situation is unique. So, if you have a question or concern that's not addressed in this book, I'm here to help. You can reach me at 978-423-2254 or shoot me an email at djlmarketing@gmail.com.

I'm confident that together we can obtain the funding necessary to create the home of your dreams.

David Lewis

CHAPTER ONE:

Renovation Lending Exists

Imagine you are on the hunt for your dream home...a place to raise a family and make memories for years to come. Everyone sets out on this search with a list of expectations and requirements. When you finally find the perfect property, it checks most of the boxes...location, number of beds/baths, attached garage, etc. However, there are a number of renovations and updates that are either necessary or desired to make this home functional and "uniquely yours." Wouldn't it be ideal if you could obtain purchase AND renovation funds in a single loan with one closing, one payment, and little money down? You can do exactly that armed with the power of renovation lending!

The Benefits of Renovation Lending

It goes without saying...homebuyers need their purchase funds when buying a property. Realistically, most houses on the market that fit within a specified budget are going to have some imperfections. Being informed about renovation loans when looking at these types of properties is very important. Not only can you obtain the purchase funds, but the renovation funds can also be included in a single loan with one closing. The convenience of one low down payment and one monthly payment is an attractive option for buyers. By obtaining purchase and renovation funds in one simple step, buyers do not have to compromise and can realistically overcome their own objections to any shortcomings when it comes to necessary updates and renovations. A renovation loan is as simple and straightforward as a conventional mortgage.

In today's housing market, competition is fierce. Homebuyers enter the market with a list of desired items that fit their lifestyle. Unfortunately, this list is going to mirror the list of everybody else searching for a potential home. The properties in great shape with an abundance of modern updates are either priced at the very top of the market or are saturated with competition because they show well. These are the homes that get snatched up rather quickly. This can lead to a lot of discouragement for anybody in the home buying market. Redirecting your focus to homes that are in your preferred location but may have some shortcomings can result in a more favorable outcome. For example, renovation lending allows you to look at homes with deferred maintenance, non-functional kitchens, no garages, lack of bedrooms, etc. They may not have instant curb appeal or may be priced below market value due to these shortcomings. Most buyers will look past these homes, not knowing that a simple renovation loan can turn the "ugly duckling" into a dream home with little to no competition from other buyers. Renovation lending can truly benefit you as the "ultimate homeowner."

In addition to these benefits, renovation lending is the cheapest way possible to finance major home renovations. There is no need to burn through hard earned savings or max out credit cards if you obtain a renovation loan. It is a well known fact that purchasing a home is going to be the largest transaction and ultimately the largest debt of your life. Preparing yourself for this type of purchase is no small undertaking. It is challenging for homebuyers to save the money needed to qualify for a home loan and come up with a down payment and closing costs. Finding extra money to fix up a home by the time it is all said and done is very difficult for most people, if not impossible. It is much more cost effective to finance the cost of these repairs in a long term, low fixed rate mortgage, than to burn through savings and credit card limits.

Lastly, the qualification process for a renovation loan is easy! People often get renovation loans confused with construction loans, which are much more difficult to qualify for. Construction loans are an entirely different animal requiring larger down payments. A renovation loan, on the other hand, is based on agency financing, either FHA or Fannie Mae. These are the government entities that put forth guidelines for the lending world. These types of loans are the easiest to qualify for due to relaxed credit standards, low down payment requirements, and not requiring multiple assets. The ease of qualification eliminates yet another common source of stress and anxiety for potential homebuyers.

Renovation Lending Misconceptions

Historically, renovation loans have developed a reputation for being "too difficult". This is a misconception. Renovation loans have been around for almost 30 years. In their infancy, they were bulky, required a lot of paperwork, and the guidelines made them very difficult to do and take longer to close. As time has gone by, changes have been made to simplify things. Professionals that specialize in renovation lending stay up to date on these changes and have been able to streamline the process. Secondly, there has been a lack of understanding not only on the consumer side, but on the side of the realtor or loan officer. They often are not armed with enough information on renovation lending to provide consumers with the knowledge they need to make informed decisions about how it could benefit the homebuying process.

Another common misconception is that people believe they are dealing with two separate loans which will require much more paperwork. As far as paperwork, a renovation loan only requires 6-8 more documents above and beyond a conventional loan. People often visualize the purchase price of the home separate from the sum of the renovations, which can certainly feel like two separate loans. In reality, these two numbers are pushed into one loan. That is where the expertise of a renovation lender comes in to be able to run the calculations and put those into one loan...one closing, one payment.

Finally, a misconception exists that renovation loans are only for major repairs as opposed to small improvements. The term "renovation" often causes people to visualize something that is in very poor condition. And though it can be used for major rehabilitation, that is not the only avenue. Many people buy a home in immaculate condition, but desire more of an open concept or different countertops. A renovation loan does not require a "gut down to the studs" renovation. It can be used for cosmetic work to simply update to personal taste.

How to Avoid Common Mistakes During the Renovation Lending Process

First and foremost, make sure you are choosing a mortgage professional with renovation lending experience. Not only should you be evaluating the individual and the experience they have executing renovation loans, but also the company they work with. Do they have a solid support staff? How efficient is the company at actually closing renovation loans? Most loan officers will tell you they know the product because they want to keep you as a client. Attempting to do one of these loans with an inexperienced loan officer will only turn into a headache and potentially destroy your chances at getting the home you have your heart set on.

Another mistake is not knowing about the option of a renovation loan before signing the purchase contract. Often, things come up after the agreement has been entered into. Perhaps the roofing does not have enough life left in it. Or the home inspector discovers health and safety violations. Unfortunately, by the time the home inspector hands you the report, the transaction is three quarters of the way done and health and safety issues can be uncovered. Several of these transactions are then forced to stop dead in their tracks and convert to a renovation loan. Switching loan programs will now delay the process significantly. All of this can be avoided by simply working with an experienced renovation lender from day one who can provide you with powerful knowledge.

Mistakes are also made when it comes to choosing the contractors to perform the work. People are accustomed to contacting many contractors and trying to secure the lowest bid. When you sign a purchase contract, you do not have the luxury of time on your side. Waiting around for too many bids can add to your timeline and potentially delay the closing. A renovation loan requires obtaining a licensed contractor prior to the close of escrow. This contractor must then provide an ironclad written estimate of materials, labor, and all work to be performed. It is also very important to choose experienced contractors. Your renovation lender will do their part to make sure the contractor is a reputable one. An inexperienced contractor may miscalculate the price of the job or be unable to complete the work in an acceptable amount of time, which again adds to delays in the timeline.

Lastly, there is such a thing as "over-improving" for your house type or location. Make sure to know your neighborhood and the styles of homes that are present. It is a mistake to do a $400,000 renovation in a $300,000 neighborhood. In order to be approved for a renovation loan, the "after improved" value must be on par with other homes in the area. If not, you would be forced to go back to the drawing board and have the contractor remove items in order to close on the home.

In conclusion, an experienced renovation lender can arm you with the information needed to turn that "fixer upper" into the home of your dreams. There is no simpler, more cost effective way to renovate than by combining purchase and renovation funds in one loan. Read on to discover tips and advice for making renovation lending work in your favor, whether you are a first time homebuyer or current homeowner.

WANT MY HELP?

"Are you ready for a complimentary, no-obligation "RENOVATION FUNDING EVALUATION?" Together we will find a solution for your specific project.

Schedule at: www.renofundingplan.com or call 978-423-2254

CHAPTER TWO:

FAQs About Renovation Lending

Q: **What kinds of things can I do to a home with renovation lending?**

A: You can make any type of renovation you wish as long as it is attached to the house. Some examples from the roof down to the foundation include roof, chimneys, siding, gutters, windows, paint, foundation repair, HVAC, plumbing, electrical, tile, flooring, etc.

The possibilities are essentially endless. You also have the power to renovate to your own taste and style by choosing items such as colors, fixtures, etc. Often times, the seller makes updates to the home to get it ready to put on the market using lower end materials or colors that they think will be appealing. A renovation loan gives the buyer the ability to change these items to align with their own personal taste.

Q: Are there limits to what I can do with renovation lending?

A: While there are many, many things that you can do to a home with a renovation loan, it is also important to understand what you cannot do. Items such as furniture, outbuildings, sheds, horse barns, landscaping, irrigation systems, etc. are all examples of luxury items that would not be funded through renovation lending.

Q: When is the renovation work able to begin?

A: The work actually is not completed until after settlement and the new buyer owns the property. With that being said, all work needs to be detailed in a written plan before settlement. On the day of the closing, the seller gets paid, the realtor commission is paid and the new buyer gets their home. Then the renovation work can officially commence.

Q: How long do I have to complete the renovations?

A: The borrower has six months from the day of closing to complete the work. As long as you are communicating with your lender about potential delays, they will allow an extension of up to twelve months. In order to obtain this extension, you must prove that there is a legit reason for the delay in work being completed (permitting issues, weather, etc.).

Q: Who can perform the work?

A: When it comes to a renovation loan, you are required to have a licensed and insured contractor. The contractor cannot be a blood relative or a company that you happen to work for. Those rules are hard and fast, and therefore very important to remember.

Q: How does the contractor get paid?

A: On a renovation loan, the contractor is paid in a simple draw process and that draw may be broken down into up to five draws depending on the type of work and how much work is being done. The contractor's money is set aside after the loan closes. As the contractor performs work, he gets paid in draws. It is a simple process but should be fully explained to the contractor so that they are comfortable and know what to expect.

Q: What is the role of the renovation loan consultant?

A: The consultant is a mandatory part of the process and is licensed by the agency. They are trained specifically to work on these types of loans. Essentially, they are acting as a quarterback in the loan process. Their role is to make sure that the work being done encompasses minimum property standards as it relates to the underwriting of your loan. Mortgage companies have many rules to abide by and oftentimes these rules are difficult to comprehend. The consultant is going to make sure that you do the required work so your home is free of health and safety violations and that you also get to include desired cosmetic updates. They keep everything together so that you can have a seamless and easy transaction on a renovation loan.

Q: How is the home appraised?

A: A home appraisal on a renovation loan is very unique in this industry. It's the only type of appraisal that happens based on "after improved state". On a traditional mortgage, the appraiser is going to go out and appraise the "as is" value. The home is listed for $300,000, the appraisal comes back for $300,000 and everything is great. With a renovation loan, the "as is" value or the sales price doesn't matter. The only thing that matters is the value of the home after the work is completed. This value is calculated by the appraiser using contractor plan specs and labor/material estimates.

Q: What is the contingency fund?

A: All renovation loans have what is called a contingency fund or a contingency reserve rule of thumb. That number is 10%-20% of the renovation costs. This fund allows extra padding in case there is an oversight once work commences. For example, if the contractor pulls down a wall and discovers a few thousand dollars of necessary plumbing repairs, the contingency fund will cover that emergency cost. In the event that the contingency fund is not needed, the money is supplied back to your principal balance like you never borrowed it at all.

Q: How can renovation lending benefit me when it comes to a home I currently own?

A: Renovation lending can be used for home refinance to include renovation funds with very little current equity. For example, if you currently own a home and have been living there for a year or two, you may begin to notice some items that need upgrades. Since you have very little equity in the home, a home equity loan to fund the desired repairs is out of the question. What many people do not realize is that a renovation loan can be used for refinance. The reason this is possible is because the loan is based off of the "after improved value", meaning we are going to project the value as if your renovation was already complete. Renovation lending is a very powerful way to make upgrades on a home with very little cash on hand or very little equity.

WANT MY HELP?

"Are you ready for a complimentary, no-obligation "RENOVATION FUNDING EVALUATION?" Together we will find a solution for your specific project.

Schedule at: www.renofundingplan.com or call 978-423-2254

CHAPTER THREE:

Getting the Home You Want

Getting the home you want comes down to how you envision your life within that home...style, amenities, bedroom counts, bathroom counts, etc. Structurally, most people are concerned with health and safety issues and whether or not utilities are in working order. At the end of the day, a priority to most people is being able to update a home to fit their personal style and "modernize" it. Nobody wants a home that will be an ongoing project. However, renovation lending allows for the home to not be exactly the way you envisioned it when you walked through the threshold and provides simple funding to make it your own.

Finding the Ideal Property

The ideal property for renovation is any property that has existed for at least one year and is lacking something you want or need. One of the biggest misconceptions when it comes to renovation purchases is that the property needs to be completely run down, ugly, scary, or have "haunted house" potential. Though you can utilize renovation lending for these types of properties, it does not have to be that extreme.

Also bear in mind that location is one thing that renovation lending CANNOT change. Be sure to choose the property based on your desired location, first and foremost. The ideal location for a renovation loan is twofold. Number one, you definitely want a location that will work for you and your lifestyle. Consider things such as proximity to work, family, amenities, shopping etc. Number two, the type of house and planned renovation needs to fit the neighborhood. In other words, the neighborhood needs to be able to absorb your vision of renovation, without your home sticking out like a sore thumb once renovation is complete. As discussed previously but worth mentioning again, the worst thing that you could do is get into a $300,000 neighborhood and do a $400,000 rehab. Over improving for your area will affect your loan and will certainly affect the value of your home.

In addition, you want to make sure that you are getting the home below market value. An easy way to accomplish this is to do some research on the neighborhood using platforms like realtor.com or Zillow and look at recent sales trends. More likely than not, any home that is in need of upgrades or repairs will already have that taken into consideration in the listing price. Any property that has solid potential and is listed slightly below market value is ideal for a renovation loan.

Determining Budget

When considering a renovation loan, your budget is going to be determined by your loan officer. They're going to look at your income, assets, debts, and overall financial picture to determine how much you can actually afford. This will give you a very raw look at your top line budget. Though most people prefer not to go straight to their top line budget because they want to have extra money for other things, it is still important to know what that number is. Start at the top and work backwards. For example, if your top line budget is $300,000, you could purchase a turnkey home that needs nothing over $300,000. Or, you could take a look at any home below $300,000 with a consideration of renovation. Keeping your top line budget in mind, you know that if you found a $150,000 home with solid potential, you would have an additional $150,000 to renovate the property. Doing a walkthrough with a licensed contractor is a great way to determine if the work that you wish to do aligns with your budget.

How Renovation Lending Can Give Home Buyers a Competitive Edge

The larger percentage of the population in the home buying market is looking for currency. They are in search of specific amenities, styles, and upgrades. Unfortunately, most people's opinions on these options are very similar. As a result, there is competition when it comes to the turnkey homes that have been recently renovated or extremely well-maintained. These types of homes appeal to the masses and bidding wars often occur. You are also more likely to end up at the top of the pricing scale for a home that is in good condition or recently rehabbed.

Armed with a renovation loan, you can now be competitive in the market by shopping for homes that have more issues on the surface. By being educated about how renovation lending works, you are going to have the upperhand on most of the homebuying population since you can visualize the potential of what a less than perfect home can be. You can have a home in your desired location, in a neighborhood that supports good value, and that is within your top line budget with little to no competition from other buyers.

Important Things to Consider After Finding the Ideal Property

When it comes to contractors, most people are accustomed to shopping around, getting bids, and choosing the company with the cheapest price. When it comes to renovation lending, cheaper is not necessarily better. A low cost contractor can often translate into subpar work. This will impact you negatively as all of the work being performed on the home goes into your equity position. You want quality contractors to increase that equity scenario and improve the quality of life for you and your family. By no means do you have to pick the most expensive contractor in the marketplace, but take the time to find one who can make your vision a reality with experience and quality craftsmanship.

Another important thing to consider is that all work to be done must be decided upon prior to the close of escrow. People often drag their feet or have trouble making up their minds when it comes to desired work. It is crucial to create a plan, execute, and stick to it in order to avoid delays in the timeline of your renovation loan.

WANT MY HELP?

"Are you ready for a complimentary, no-obligation "RENOVATION FUNDING EVALUATION?" Together we will find a solution for your specific project.

Schedule at: www.renofundingplan.com
or call 978-423-2254

CHAPTER FOUR:

How to Talk to Your Realtor About Renovation Lending

Many new home buyers view their realtor as a trusted advisor selected based upon social proof (often a referral from a friend, family member, or co-worker). The assumption for many buyers is that their realtor will know how to guide them through every aspect of the real estate market. When it comes to renovation lending, this is often untrue. The vast majority of the realtor population remains uneducated on how the process works and how renovation lending can help buyers get exactly what they need. This is certainly not to say that all realtors are uneducated or unwilling to work with this type of product, but by and large, that is the consensus. So, having this knowledge upfront as a buyer prior to shopping for a home is very important when interviewing potential realtors. Aim for a deep discussion about what your goals are when it comes to renovation lending and make sure that the realtor can help you reach those goals. If your realtor knows you are interested in a renovation loan, they can help you look for a property that is less than your top of the line budget, as discussed in previous chapters. Your realtor can also help research repairs or updates the home needs and how to go about getting those priced. They may be able to provide contractor contacts that can provide walk-throughs and estimates.

To find out if the realtor you are considering is a good fit, a simple conversation is all it takes. First, is the realtor willing and open to work with a renovation loan transaction? While renovation loans don't take terribly long, they can take a bit longer than standard purchase contracts. Therefore, the realtor needs to be willing to negotiate a contract that is a minimum of two weeks longer than the standard 30 days...generally, a 45 day contract. In addition, the realtor needs to be able to "leave their ego at the door" and get on the phone with a renovation lending professional to re-acquaint themselves or better understand the process. This will alleviate any stress throughout the transaction that may fall on the buyer. A realtor who has an open mind and excellent communication skills is a must.

Your renovation lending professional can steer you towards realtors who will have your best interest in mind. A dedicated, knowledgeable, and well-experienced loan professional will have close relationships with realtors who are not only open to this type of transaction, but that understand the process thoroughly so they can guide you, step by step. Reversely, if you happen to be working with a realtor first and decide that renovation lending is the best option for you, your realtor may refer you to a lending professional. It is important to make sure that the lender has a vast knowledge base and experience with renovation lending.

At the end of the day, if you find a realtor trying to talk you OUT of a renovation loan, they do not have your best interest in mind. Don't be intimidated. If you are confident that a renovation loan can make your visions come true, stand your ground politely and be firm. If a realtor doesn't feel comfortable with a certain product, they will not often admit it. Instead, they may try to push their expertise on you in another area that deters from renovation lending. The truth of the matter is, for anyone purchasing a less than perfect home, renovation lending is a powerful, beneficial tool.

WANT MY HELP?

"Are you ready for a complimentary, no-obligation "RENOVATION FUNDING EVALUATION?" Together we will find a solution for your specific project.

Schedule at: www.renofundingplan.com or call 978-423-2254

CHAPTER FIVE:

Renovation Lending for Your

Current Home

The main reason for you as a current homeowner to consider a renovation loan over a regular refinance or equity line is not having enough equity in the home to cover the costs of the desired renovation. In addition, it is not in your best financial interest to finance renovations on high interest credit cards. Keep in mind that renovation loans are based on the FUTURE value upon renovation completion, NOT the current value. This is one of the biggest secrets about this type of lending that most people are unaware of. It is also important to remember that you still have to qualify like you would for any other mortgage. Factors like financial standing, credit, income, and employment are still very relevant. When all of your ducks are in a row, renovation lending becomes the BEST way to finance improvements on your current home.

Renovation Lending vs. Refinance

One of the most common questions I receive from current homeowners is "Can I perform a renovation loan as a refinance?" The answer is "Yes, you can! And you should!" There are a couple of substantial benefits for using the loan in this way. First of all, as mentioned above, you are able to access more equity than with any other form of traditional financing. This is because we base the loan off of the future value of the home according to the renovations you are going to complete. Secondly, in any interest rate market over the past two decades, renovation lending is STILL more cost effective than any consumer style loan or credit cards that can be used to finance the desired repairs. It is spread out over a longer period of time. Renovation loans are consistent in their ability to be the most cost effective, simple solutions to making your home the way you want it.

Tips for Using Renovation Lending on Your Current Home

The first step is to consider what you really want to accomplish with the home. Though a renovation loan can be used for repairs such as roofing, heating, new siding, windows, etc., it can be used for SO much more. Often, growing families fall in love with their home. They like the neighborhood, the school system, and the proximity to family and amenities. However, they realize as the family expands that they are lacking space. A renovation loan CAN be used to add square footage! You have the ability to build the home out, add second levels, create additional bathrooms, bedrooms, and expand great rooms. With that being said, you still want to consider the value of other homes in the neighborhood and not "over-improve" for your area. The neighborhood needs to be able to "absorb" the style and size of the home you wish to create. Otherwise, you may not get enough money even based on future value to create your vision if that vision is outside the scope of the neighborhood. In addition, it is beneficial to call or visit your local planning and zoning department to make sure there are no restrictions as far as the size of the home, lot lines, etc. A quick verification regarding your plans with the local municipality is a great place to start before you dive in.

When it comes to choosing a contractor, since you don't have a purchase contract and are not against the clock, you can be more selective when choosing who you want to perform the work. Take the time to do a little research and make sure you are getting the most value and experience for the money. Establish a good rapport and make sure you are both on the same page when it comes to the scope of work. The more information that a contractor can provide as far as plans, dimensions, etc., the better. This will improve the likelihood of the "after-improved" value being as high as possible. Be prepared with the right professionals and create a "dream team" to share in your vision for the home.

WANT MY HELP?

"Are you ready for a complimentary, no-obligation "RENOVATION FUNDING EVALUATION?" Together we will find a solution for your specific project.

Schedule at: www.renofundingplan.com or call 978-423-2254

DO YOU HAVE A QUESTION FOR DAVID?

If you have more questions about funding a home through renovation lending, then let me know. I'm happy to talk with you and help you to evaluate your unique situation.

Phone

978-423-2254

Email

djlmarketing@gmail.com

About David Lewis

David has spent the past 25 years working in the mortgage industry. His superpowers come from helping literally thousands of families successfully navigate through the renovation loan process. David's years of experience and unsurpassed knowledge of renovation lending have given him the unique ability to elevate the renovation lending customer experience well above industry standards.

Born and raised in Massachusetts, David Lewis now resides in the state of Connecticut with his beautiful wife, Gina, and their awesome Blue French Bulldog, Sir Maxximus Blu.

EMAIL: djlmarketing@gmail.com

LINKEDIN:
https://www.linkedin.com/in/djlmarketing/

FACEBOOK:
https://www.facebook.com/RenovationMortgageExpert/

PHONE: (978) 423-2254

What David's Clients are Saying

I would like to express my sincere appreciation for all that you did for me throughout the loan process. Being there for me, to take or return my call, at a moment's notice provided me with the reassurance and trust that everything that needed to get done would get completed. I appreciate you and your team keeping me informed throughout the process.

Buying this home and getting a renovation loan is completely different from what I remember when I bought my house 15 years ago. Working with a team so knowledgeable made me feel comfortable and confident knowing that I was working with someone who was the best in the business.

I will certainly be sharing my experience with my family and friends and trust that if/when someone I know decides to renovate their home, they'll turn to you and your team.

Nikki Wayne

I wanted to write you a quick note and let you know how satisfied Lisa and I are with the whole renovation loan process. From the very beginning you were honest and explained this to us in a way we could easily understand. Frankly the process was fun and exciting. I would highly recommend your services to anyone interested in a renovation loan of their own. Lisa and I both look forward to working with you in the future if the opportunity were to come.

I hope you enjoyed your holidays and Happy New Year.

Andrew Goff and Lisa Cavalier

We knew we wanted to buy a "fixer upper" but got shut down everywhere we looked. Banks wouldn't loan us money for the house and the renovation, but then a close friend introduced us to David. He explained all of our options, and we all decided a 203k renovation loan was best for us.

From there David clearly laid out all of the steps that needed to be completed and what he would need from us to complete the loan application/paperwork. He made the process effortless and let us pay more attention to getting the home we wanted.

Without a renovation loan there's no doubt that we wouldn't have been able to have the home we do. There's also no doubt that without David, this process wouldn't have been nearly as enjoyable.

Thanks David!

Tommy and Ashley Coughlin

www.ingramcontent.com/pod-product-compliance
Lightning Source LLC
Chambersburg PA
CBHW070908210326
41521CB00010B/2112